© 2020 Tom Huth

Published by
Sungold Editions
Santa Barbara

ISBN: 978-0-9991678-4-7

Cover Photo: Marta Ortigosa

In the Time of Corona

Poems by Tom Huth

Sungold Editions
2020

Contents

Greetings from Afar	6
The Passage	8
Tensions on the Trail	10
It's Our Call	12
Gratitude	14
Sweatpants	16
What Day Is It?	18
Taming Summer	20
Face Time	22
Welcoming Uncertainty	24
Up in the Air	26
Dear Doctor Fauci	28
Coronavirus Knows	30
A Fresh Start	32
For Sale	34
Lonely in Here	36
History Now	38
One Fabulous Month	40
Gifts of Intimacy	42
Root Root Root	44

Routines	46
Untouchables	48
In the Bubble	50
The Human Touch	52
What We Don't Know	54
How It Used to Be	56
Death March	58
Between Realities	60
Caution and Kin	62
Herd Immunity	64
Facelift	66
Play Ball!	68
Drinking Outdoors	70
An Empty House	72
What Was a School?	74
Your Digital Likeness	76
Evanescence	78
Let Us Grieve	80
Pod Me Up	82
The Seasons of Our Lives	84

Greetings from Afar

I wander the empty streets
the one freedom I'm allowed
my mask fogging my glasses
and inciting a furious itch
on my nose which Dr. Fauci
implores me not to scratch

A potential Covid spreader
approaches on the sidewalk
Should I cross the street?
    She veers into
    the bike lane

I can't tell if she has a face
behind her bandanna and shades
but we exchange muffled hellos
    as will happen these days

When we get our lives back
will I still greet strangers
as if I long to be friends?

The Passage

If we think of the plague
as a crisis then our goal is
to return as soon as possible
to the lives we lived before

If we treat it as a passage
we'll see beyond the familiar
and glimpse new opportunities
to engage our boundless souls

We give up all expectations
of where a passage will lead
If we know what's coming
it won't be a passage

The future is up for grabs
Will we go back to normal?
Or can we leverage the moment
to aim for a yet larger life?

Tensions on the Trail

Hiking a perfect escape
from Covid and boredom
surrendering to nature
instead of confinement

I get directions online
for Bear Mountain Trail
then notice the reviews

Two days ago
> *Super crowded*
> *Prepare to get*
> *close to people*

Yesterday
> *Hikers yelling*
> *at people not*
> *wearing masks*

This morning
> *Tensions high*
> *hikers shaming*
> *the unmasked*

I think I'll stay home
play online solitaire
download that new
    meditation app

It's Our Call

When the lockdown ends will we
dance in the streets like Vikings
heralding the return of the sun
from the long night of winter?

Will we go to the movies
as soon as they open?
flock to restaurants?
that cozy corner bar?
a heavy-breathing gym?
stroll into a barbershop?
open wide for a dentist?

Will we hug each other
as soon as it's sanctioned
or will we give it a while?
Will it be a lusty embrace
     or a pat on the back?

Whatever the doctors
and Trumpsters decide
    it's our call

GRATITUDE

Surely we learn more
in times of struggle
than on cruise control

Plainly adversity
can help us realize
our highest selves

We inherit fortitude
from the worst things
that ever befell us

Thank you Covid
for lifting us
to new heights
of gratitude
for the joys
we have left

Sweatpants

How many of you wear the same
clothes day after day because
you don't get out of the house?

How many of you are taking
fewer showers because who can
smell you from six feet away?

Do you bother combing your hair?
Do you fancy the caveman look?
Do you wear slippers all day?

How many of you secretly enjoy
the relaxed pace of hermitage
the fewer plans
     fewer choices
          fewer distractions
               fewer obligations?

Is hermitage destined
to change who we are?

What Day Is It?

Saturday?   Wednesday?
Sunday?   Last Tuesday?
In the time of corona
they're all the same

Weekends once a celebration
our respite from servitude
picnics potlucks parties
cocktails cookouts concerts

Now the lines blur between
working and playing
   home and office
      one day and the next
         sickness and health

Orders and guidelines shave
the highlights off our weeks
cast a sameness over our days
sedate us with precautions
gloves wipes masks sanitizers
flattening our spontaneity
the days expiring unnoticed
a springtime without rebirth
only one note on the calendar
     take out the trash
and begin again

TAMING SUMMER

Let's strike a bargain with God
He will give us our lives back
if we agree to tone things down

We will get to have a summer
but it won't be quite the same
trading the larks of intimacy
for a pocket full of prudence

We will get to see our friends
but without the lavish dinners
the welcoming hugs and kisses
the passing of cannabis pipes

We will parade on the 4th of July
in personal protective equipment
with nobody lining the route

We will creep back into public
but it won't be quite the same
Doubt will be along for the ride

Am I being too bold?
    keeping enough distance?
        Or am I letting fear
            take charge again?

FACE
TIME

They keep telling us
Don't touch your face

I do it by instinct
to reassure myself
I'm still here

I try my best
   to keep my hands
      in my lap
But then oops!
   I lose focus
      scratch my chin

I itch
therefore
I am

How do you
keep track
of yourself
these days?

Or is that
the least
of your
worries?

Welcoming Uncertainty

Patrick Henry proclaimed
    Give me certainty
    or give me death
At least those would be
his sentiments if he had
to live with this plague

Certainty is our refuge
our release from angst
our wager against ruin
our stock in our dreams
our illusion of a future
Now we have no certainty

Will there be a second wave?
Will they find a vaccine?
A third wave? A fourth wave?
Will next summer be normal?
Will this always be with us?
Questions blowing in the wind

If we could find a way
to welcome uncertainty
we'd be free to enjoy
what is happening now
    As we liked to say
    back in the day
    Go with the flow

Up in the Air

When will it be safe to fly?
Should I postpone my wedding?
When will I see my children?
Should I move to New Zealand?
When will yoga studios open?
When did the moon disappear?

Is it safe to touch door knobs?
Is it safe to touch my mail?
Is it okay to breathe deeply?
Is it safe to touch money?
Is it safe to touch groceries?
When did the stars disappear?

Are my handlebars infected?
Can I catch it from babies?
Can I touch my steering wheel?
Why is my hair falling out?
Can I pet my son's puppy?
Why am I wetting my pants?

Dear Doctor Fauci

Dear Doctor Fauci
I have an ouchie
and I'm certain
what's hurtin'
is my mounting fear
that our Leader Dear
is about to make
a tragic mistake

Dear Doctor Fauci
I am beyond grouchy
If Trump ends our shelter
it'll be helter-skelter
Folks will get reckless
He will turn feckless
Tens of thousands will die
He'll be pie in the sky
and our only consolation
will be the coronation
of Joe Biden to save us
from this raging ignoramus

Coronavirus Knows

Oh coronavirus
why do you work
in devious ways?

Why do you take
little naps
now and then?

Why do you let us
return to being
busy bees sooner
than we should?

Oh coronavirus
you know how
hard it will
be to return
to our caves
once we behold
sunshine again

How can it be
you know us
better than we
know ourselves?

A Fresh Start

Old assumptions swept away
we face a magnificent void
begging to be repopulated
by figments of reinvention

It's like when I was widowed
reaching the end of one path
and heading out on the next
no signs pointing the way

When the destination is unknown
anxiety plays sidekick to hope
The time of corona invites us
      to set out on the journey

For Sale

29 million doses
of the wonder drug
hydroxychloroquine
as seen on Fox News
and The Trump Show

    Never used
    Brand name
    Game Changer

Side effects include
 irregular heartbeat
  irritability
   hallucinations
    constipation
     shortness of breath
    compulsive lying
   habitual bullying
  self-adulation
 self-victimization
toxic defensiveness
absence of empathy

Cash only
No refunds
D.J. Trump
1600 Pennsylvania Avenue

Lonely in Here

Men in masks used to scare me
Now I avoid men without masks

Inside my mask I'm a lonely guy
Nobody is able to see the smile
I have spent my life perfecting
to advertise my best intentions

When I walk past people
can they see the crinkles
of warmth and camaraderie
at the corners of my eyes?

Not likely from 6 feet away

We've been disappeared
  by the corona witness
    protection program

HISTORY NOW

We are privileged
to be living out
American history

The deadliest health
calamity in a century

The worst economic
collapse since the
fall of Mesopotamia

The most promising
protests for justice
since the Sixties

The worst federal
leadership since
Van Buren botched
The Panic of 1837

Playing out
   all at once
      before our
         eyes agog

ONE FABULOUS MONTH

I try to explain to my son
We will have to redistance
    What does that mean?
It means people have to stay
apart from each other again
    Can I still cuddle you?
The numbers have gotten worse

Little Tommy starts to cry
    I want to cuddle!
Even if it makes you sick?
    You wouldn't make me sick
I could if I was sick myself
    Would Mommy make me sick?
Not on purpose she wouldn't
He is crying harder
I have a way with children

Listen up now Little Tommy
We grown-ups blew it big time
We didn't flatten the curve
We went to the mall instead
parties bars beaches rallies
out for ice cream every night
June was a super-duper month
But now we have to hide again
    only better than before

Gifts
of
Intimacy

Imagine our appreciation
for life's casual favors
after this reign of fear
and sacrifice
      has run
           its course
                at last

In isolation we store up
our appetite for intimacy
When we can touch again
we'll be doubly nourished
for having been denied

Banning affection
   the surest way
   to sanctify it

**Root
Root
Root**

Lock me out of the ballgame
just dispose of the crowd
play your mock season in solitude
guarantee that you'll never get booed

Let us root root root for a vaccine
to save Mike Trout and his crew
for it's one
       two
           three strikes you're out
           in the I.C.U.

We'll keep watching on TV
Still it won't be the same
no spitting no fighting saliva tests
masks in the dugouts
and temperature checks

Let us root root root for a vaccine
if Mike Trout dies it's a shame
for it's one
       two
           three strikes he's off
           to the Hall of Fame

ROUTINES

When the plague is aprowl
when our lifeboat-of-state
is listing toward loonybin
our daily routines steady us
give us something to count on

My habits nothing special
read the paper eat a muffin
open the Macbook take a walk
But they grant familiarity
ground me in an allegiance
with what is already known

Routines lull me
     into believing
          I have it all
               under control

Untouchables

Americans used to feel
welcomed around the world
our presidents courted
our tourist dollars prized
Now we are global pariahs

The Aussies won't let us in
The Kiwis slammed the door
The Canucks shut the border
The Nigerians won't take us
The Cambodians don't want us
Even the Cape Verde Islanders

Itching to make it to Europe?
The E.U. will send you back
They're glad to see people
from Rwanda Serbia Andorra
Algeria San Marino Uruguay
Tunisia Monaco Montenegro
     even China
     But not us

Uncle Sam is Typhoid Mary
     what we deserve
     for walling out
     hungry immigrants

In the Bubble

The plague draws
us toward those
we have trusted
for the longest
because you never
know with newbies
whom they have seen
where they have been
what they have touched

At one time bubbles
were just bubbles
> *I'm forever*
> *blowing bubbles*
> *pretty bubbles*
> *in the air*

Now they are havens
protective umbrellas
cloisters of exclusion
clusters of xenophobia
political sanctuaries
hideouts from reality
guarantors of innocence
shelters from the storm

The Human Touch

My old friend Sharon telephones
her voice brimming with emotion
    Tommy could you help me?
    I think Molly is dying

I mask up and walk down the hill
her poodle lying in the driveway
We roll her onto a blanket
    carry her into the garage
        lay her gently on her bed

Sharon's eyes glassy with tears
Molly her comrade for 17 years
since just after Jim passed away
    Thanks Tommy
Do you want me to stay?
    I'll just sit with her
She stands gazing at Molly
I place a comforting hand
on her back and we embrace
and it feels so right after
going without the human touch
for longer than we could bear

An hour later we pick up
the blanket again and carry
a peaceful Molly to the car
for her last ride to town

What We Don't Know

This virus is so novel
we don't even know what
we don't know about it

Why do some people die
while most go scot-free?

If you get infected
will you be immune
and for how long?

If a vaccine works
on only some people
how do you know if
you're one of them?

Why was there a viral spike
after Trump's Tulsa rally
but not after the protests
for George Floyd's murder?

Was it just being outdoors
or is it foolish to wonder
if moral clarity
     can confer immunity?

How
It
Used
to
Be

Mommy what was a store?
It's where we used to shop
Like Amazon?
No a building we went into
Why did you do that?
Well if I wanted a special dress
I could see it with my own eyes
instead of just on the screen
I could touch it with my hands
and try it on in a fitting room
What was a fitting room?
It doesn't matter anymore honey
What was a special dress for?
Because we could leave our houses
to be with people and go to parties
What were parties?
Where friends came together to share
laughs and good food and happy drinks
That sounds like so much fun
Oh it sure was honey
Now say your prayers
to President Bezos
and I'll tuck you in

DEATH MARCH

Imagine one week before the election
families of corona victims marching
on Washington by the tens of thousands

Widows widowers
   daughters sons
      mothers fathers
         black Americans
           white Americans
              brown Americans
walking past the White House
  in deadly silence with signs
     bearing photos of loved ones
        killed by cruel indifference

Sixty thousand Americans
   wearing black face masks
      parading in single file
         distanced 6 feet apart
           A week-long procession
               from Baltimore to D.C.
                  igniting the emotions
                     of a spellbound world

BETWEEN REALITIES

We presumed we would return to normal
Then we fancied it being a new normal
Now normal is gone from the playbook
We sense there might be no returning

We are floating free

   between the reality

      of a faraway past

         and a new reality

            scarcely revealed

Caution
and
Kin

The virus makes us wary
of those we would like
to wrap our arms around

My stepson and his family
are driving through Colorado
and want to stop for a visit

I haven't been with my kids
since Covid came a-knocking
Do I let them into my house?
I don't let other people in

Some friends keep six feet
from their grown children
But most will not abide
such unholy restrictions
Kinship trumps discretion

Will my visitors
     be as leery of me
          as I am of them?

Herd
Immunity

If we can't change our habits
if half of us won't mask up
will there be a tipping point?
If the virus keeps spreading
will a dark vision prevail?

> *Rip off your face masks*
> *Sleep with the infected*
> *Let's all charge ahead*
> *toward herd immunity!*

Countless millions would die
so that those who remained
could come out of the shadows
     (according to the theory)
and the economy could thrive
     (until immunity wore off)

Too bleak?
Maybe we'll change our ways
Maybe deniers will believe
Maybe immunity is forever
Maybe Trump is our prophet
and it will just disappear

If a menace is novel how can
we dismiss any conclusion?

FACELIFT

Happiness once drew upon many sources
contentment loving family and friends
right livelihood rewarding travels
Now all I ask is a decent face mask

I try hospital-blue 50-in-a-box
polypropylene masks from China
but every time I open my mouth
they pull down off of my nose

I try a stylish outlaw bandanna
It too slips down no matter how
tightly I tie the fucking knot

Then this internet ad
    adjustable ear straps
    two layers of protection
    moisture-wicking cotton
    infused with copper and zinc
    to kill odor-causing microbes
And a cone for the nose
plus a cup for the chin

I ignore the disclaimer absolving
the seller in the event of my death
because I love the charcoal gray
Hey everybody look at my new mask!
A facelift for the time of corona

Play Ball!

Three days into the new season
18 Miami Marlins test positive
18 replacements are dragooned
and the team returns to action
    if action means playing
    before a few dummy fans
    made out of cardboard
Now the Cards are quarantined
haven't played in two weeks
But they'll rally to the cause
play double-headers every day

The country is in freefall
still the games must go on
The owners need to make it
through October to cash in
on the TV playoff jackpot

Basketball and hockey are back
players imprisoned in bubbles
without families without lives

Picture Game 7 of the NBA finals
played in an empty Cloroxed arena
before a global video audience
while in the streets outside
the sick and homeless and hungry
scrabble for the few scraps left

DRINKING
OUTDOORS

What would windbags do
if we couldn't drink
with each other outside?

Fear of transmission frees
hosts from old civilities
No need to feed friends
to check unwatched pots
to keep track of who is
grain-free or potato-free
or allergic to zucchini

We put out coronasafe snacks
Guests bring their own drinks
After two hours they go home
and we're not stuck
    with a sink full
        of dirty dishes

Yet autumn nears
and we have no
cold-weather plan

An Empty House

I stand alone in my kitchen
looking around the house
we built when we were young
and I picture the good times

I see us in the dining nook
cozied shoulder to shoulder
with our fondest of friends
getting Rocky Mountain high

    the nook now silent
    not used all summer

I see us in the window seat
telling jokes sharing hopes
confessing transgressions
the ghosts of parties past

    the view still divine
    only me to take it in

I don't enter your house now
and you don't step into mine
Yet I keep the place tidy
in case they find a vaccine

    as if those good times
    could ever be restored

What
Was
A
School?

Mommy what was a restaurant?
Where lots of people ate together
and you had to shout to be heard
 What was a movie theater?
A dark room where strangers crowded
side-by-side to see the same films
 Mommy what was a school?
A building where hundreds of kids
squeezed in to watch teachers talk
 What was an airplane?
A flying tube full of super-spreaders
hoping for better luck somewhere else
 Mommy I'm tired of not going
 anywhere or seeing anybody
 except Weird Uncle Harry
 and having our stuff
 delivered by robots
Honey the robots they send now
treat women with such respect
I hardly miss human beings
 I get lonely Mommy
 Don't you get lonely?
People learn to adapt
That is our nature
 Mommy what is nature?
Let's save that for another time

Your Digital Likeness

This might be a blow
    to your self-esteem
but your physical presence
    no longer matters
Your digital likeness
    will do just fine

Whether you work at home
or consult your doctors
or attend a conference
or see your therapist
or talk to your kids
your image on Zoom
not only suffices
but excels since
it's not likely
to kill anyone

If your physical presence
will not be required soon
you are advised to put it
in storage until the time
of your next video meetup

EVANESCENCE

In the time of corona
the days streak past

Every Friday when
I water the plants
I ask *Didn't I do
this just yesterday?*

Every Wednesday
at the grocery I'm
Judy Collins *Where
does the time go?*

With less to do
some days seem
never-ending

Still they vanish
so quickly I gauge
my life shortening
    week by week

Let Us Grieve

Look at all that we've lost
untold legions of loved ones
jobs and financial security
confidence in our democracy
more black people murdered
Let us grieve for our nation
Let us grieve for ourselves

We who survive have lost
certainty about tomorrow
the solaces of intimacy
faith in our institutions
days never to be returned
Let us take time to mourn

When I hear Obama address
the convention I cry aloud
for the beauty of his vision
for the humanity in his voice
for the love that is missing
from the heart of our nation

**POD
ME
UP**

Widower aged 68 Capricorn
looking for a pod to join
Will quarantine for 21 days
and do dishes on weekends

Full disclosure
Got booted out of last pod
for going to a strip show
although it was outdoors
and the girls were masked
      from stem to stern

Looking for youthful pod
with progressive politics
paleo-opportunivore diet
5G wireless covered parking

Will do dishes on weekends
Did I already mention that?
      Prefer pod with
      memory wing

The Seasons of Our Lives

These are the seasons of our lives
a counterfeit summer stealing away
the virus shadowing our every move
a time of feeling newly vulnerable
long after we thought we'd be free

These are the seasons of our lives
the days out my window shortening
the sunset marching cruelly south
so many stout souls growing weary
of inhibitions and deprivations
even as the next wave approaches

These are the seasons of our lives
the aspens turning early this year
our Labor Day parties called off
our Halloween trick-or-treating
Aunt Rose's Thanksgiving dinner
department-store Santa Clauses

These are the seasons of our lives
By winter back into hibernation
By spring queuing for vaccines
By summer standing 3 feet closer
By autumn getting one hug a week
By '22 taking off our masks
   and stashing them away
      for the next surprise

www.ingramcontent.com/pod-product-compliance
Lightning Source LLC
Chambersburg PA
CBHW010447010526
44118CB00021B/2536